# *For Michael*

*Name:* _____

*Birthdate:* _____

*Hometown:* _____

*Nickname:* _____

*Background:* _____

_____

_____

*Highlights and achievements:* _____

_____

_____

_____

_____

_____

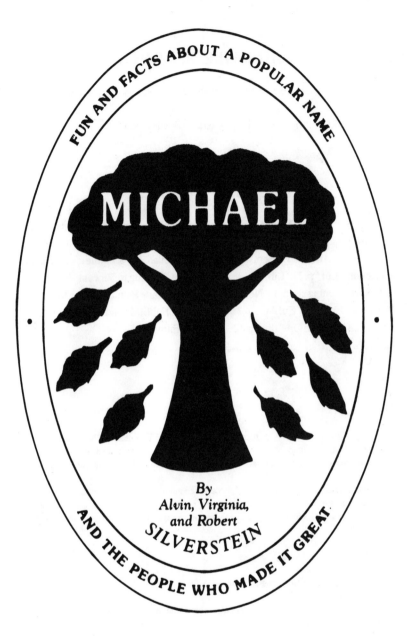

FUN AND FACTS ABOUT A POPULAR NAME

# MICHAEL

By
Alvin, Virginia,
and Robert
SILVERSTEIN

AND THE PEOPLE WHO MADE IT GREAT

# AVSTAR Publishing Corporation

P.O. Box 537, Lebanon, NJ 08833
Tel.: (908) 236-6210

# ACKNOWLEDGMENTS

The authors would like to thank all those who kindly supplied photos and information.

Thanks, too, to our capable typesetter, Shelley Remaly of Mountaintop Typesetting.

# PICTURE CREDITS

p.10: Just Born; p.13: Michael Caine; p.15: Michael Crichton; p.17: Massachusetts Executive Department; p.18: AP/Wide World Photo; p.20: AP/Wide World Photo; p.21: ProServ, Andrew D. Bernstein; p.23: The Philadelphia Phillies; p.26: Timic Productions Ltd; p.27: Library of Congress; p.29: Edgar Vincent Associates; p.30: Soviet Embassy; p.31: New York Public Library Picture Collection; p.34: CBS Records, Chris Cuffaro; p.36: New York Public Library Picture Collection; p. 38: Robert Opalsky; p.42: Scimitar Films Ltd.

The authors and publisher have carefully researched numerous sources to ensure the accuracy and completeness of the information in this book, but we assume no responsibility for any errors or omissions. Any apparent slights against people or organizations mentioned in *MICHAEL*, are unintentional.

Manufactured in the United States of America

Library of Congress Cataloging-in-Publication Data
Silverstein, Alvin.
    Michael : fun and facts about a popular name and the people who made it great / by Alvin, Virginia, and Robert Silverstein.
    p.   cm.
    Summary: Presents anecdotes, trivia, and puzzles relating to the name Michael, its origin and lore, and provides brief sketches of notable people and fictitious characters with the name or one of its variants.
    ISBN 0-9623653-6-X : $11.95. — ISBN 0-9623653-7-8 (pbk.) : $4.95
    1. Michael (Name)—Miscellanea—Juvenile literature. [1. Michael (Name) 2. Names, Personal.]
I. Silverstein, Virginia B. II Silverstein, Robert, 1959- . III. Title.
CS2391.M5S54 1990
929.4'4—dc20          90-80673          CIP          AC

# CONTENTS

# 1. A POPULAR NAME

## What's in a Name?

Your name is one of the most personal things you have. You look up when you hear it called. The sound or sight of your name may make friends and family think of you. You might find it hard to imagine being called anything else.

Although a name is personal, there are others who share it. If your name is Michael, for example, there may be other Michaels in the neighborhood, at school, or at work. There are Michaels in books and in the news; popular comic strips and TV shows have characters named Michael. Have you ever wondered about those other people who share your name? Are they like you in other ways, too?

## Michael Is a Popular Name

If your name is Michael, you have plenty of company. Michael has been the most popular name for baby boys in the United States for more than twenty-five years. In other countries, it is also a very popular name. Each language has its own way of saying "Michael": *Michel* in French, for example, *Miguel* in Spanish, and *Mikhail* in Russian.

## The Meaning of Michael

People pick names for babies for many reasons. They may want to name a child after a famous person or a relative. Perhaps they choose a name for its meaning. Or they may just like the way it sounds.

*Michael* is a Biblical name. It comes from Hebrew words meaning "Who is like God." The first Michael was an angel, who protected the Israelites.

## Famous Michaels

There have been many famous Michaels in all areas of life. Kings, presidents, and other world leaders have borne this name. Michaels have been leaders in business and sports. They have made great discoveries in science and created beautiful art and music. Writers and philosophers named Michael have shown us new ways to look at the world, and entertainers have made us laugh and cry.

In the chapters that follow, you'll find out more about this popular name, Michael, and the interesting and unusual people who share it.

# 2. ABOUT THE NAME MICHAEL

## The First Michaels

Michael is a very old name. The ancient Latin and Greek forms were taken from an even older Hebrew name, **Mikhael** (pronounced mee-kha-EHL), which means "Who is like God." Another Hebrew name, **Mikha** (or **Micah**), has the same meaning. So does the feminine version, **Michal**.

Both Mikhael and Micah were popular names among the ancient Israelites. Some parents chose the name for its meaning—naming a child Mikhael was a way of showing their love and respect for God. Others named their children after other Michaels in the family or after famous Michaels in the Bible.

In both the Jewish and Christian religions, Michael is an important name. Mikhael was the angel who protected the Israelites in the Old Testament, and Micah was a prophet. Michal was the wife of King David. In the New Testament, Michael is the archangel, or the head of all the angels.

## The History of "Michael"

Michael was a common name in England from the 12th century until the 16th century. (At that time it was pronounced more like the French Michel, "Mee-SHEHL.")

7

Later it was common in Greece and in Slavic-speaking countries. It was also popular in Ireland from the 17th century on. Irish immigrants who came to America in the 19th century brought the name Michael with them.

By 1950, Michael had become so popular in the United States, Canada, and England that it replaced John as the number one name in many polls. Ever since then, Michael has remained one of the most popular names in the United States, as well as in other countries such as Canada, England, France, and Germany.

## "Michael" Around the World

The Michaels of today's world make up a sort of family or clan. They all share the same first name, although they might not recognize that name if they heard it in another country. Different peoples each have their own way of saying and spelling "Michael."

In France, in the French-speaking parts of Canada, and in other French-speaking countries of the world, Michaels are called **Michel** (pronounced mee-SHEHL). In Spain, and in Mexico, Central and South America, **Miguel** (mee-GEHL) is a popular name as well. **Mikhail** (mee-kha-EHL) is the way they say "Michael" in the Soviet Union, and **Michele** (mee-SHEHL-leh) in Italy. **Mick** and **Mickey** are Irish variations, and **Miles, Mitch,** and **Mitchell** are English.

Forms of Michael are also popular girls' names. These include the English **Michelle** (from the French **Michèle**), **Micki, Midge,** and **Michaela**, the Italian **Micaela** and **Mia**, and the Spanish **Miguela** and **Miguelita**.

## A Dictionary of Michaels

*MICAH* (MYE-ka): from **Hebrew** *Micaiah*, "Who is like God?"
*MICHAEL* (MYE-k'l): **Latin** and **Greek** forms, from **Hebrew** *Mikhael*, "Who is like God?"
*MICK, MICKEY, MICKY:* **Irish** nicknames.
*MIKE:* usual nickname for Michael in **English**.
*MILES:* from **French** forms, *Mihiel* and *Miel;* also probably from **Old German** *Milo,* meaning "generous," or **Latin** *Miles*, "soldier."
*MISCHA* (MEE-sha): **Slavic** nickname.
*MITCHELL* (MITCH-'l): **Middle English** form from **Hebrew** *Mikhal;* or from a word meaning "big"; popular as a surname; *MITCH:* nickname.

## Michaels Around the World

**Basque:** Mikel (mee-kehl)
**Czech:** Michal
**Danish:** Michael (MEE-chehl), Mikael, Mikkel (MEE-kel)
**Dutch:** Michiel, Micheltje
**English:** Michael (MYE-k'l), Mickel, Mickey, Mickie, Micky, Mike, Miles, Milo, Mitch, Mitchel, Mitchell, Myles
**French:** Michau (mee-SHOW), Michel (mee-SHEL), Michon
**Gaelic:** Micheil (MEECH-yell)
**German:** Michael (mee-KHAH-ehl), Micha, Michel, Misha
**Greek:** Michael
**Hungarian:** Mihaly, Mika, Misi (MEE-shee), Miska (MEESH-ka)
**Irish:** Michael, Micheal (mee-HAHL), Mick
**Israeli:** Micha (MEE-shah), Michal, Micha-el (mee-shah-EHL), Michel
**Italian:** Michele (mee-SHEHL-leh)
**Norwegian:** Mikkel (MIK-el)
**Polish:** Michal
**Portuguese:** Miguel
**Russian:** Mikhail (mee-kha-EHL), Mischa, Misha, Mishe, Mishenka
**Scottish:** Michael, Micheil
**Spanish:** Miguel (mee-GEHL), Miguelito
**Swedish:** Mikael (mee-KHAHL), Mikas, Mikel

## Michael as a Last Name

Long ago, people had only one name. But some names, such as Michael or John, were very common. There might be five or ten Michaels living in the same village. How could people know which one was meant? They used phrases like "Michael Long-Nose" or "Michael John's-Son." Gradually, these phrases turned into last names.

Since so many people were named Michael, forms of the name also became common last names. In fact, hundreds of surnames around the world came from Michael. Some of the most common mean "Michael's son," said in different ways in various languages—for example, the English **Michaelson,** Danish **Michelson,** German **Michelsen,** Norwegian **Michaelsen** and **Mikkelsen,** Scottish **McMichael,** Swedish **Mickelsson,** and Russian **Mikhailov.**

Other common Michael last names include: **Michael, Michaels, Michels, Mitchell, Mix,** and **Mixon** which came from England, **Michel, Michelin, Michelet,** and **Michaud** from France, **Michaelis** from Germany, **Mikos** from Greece, **Miceli, Micelli,** and **Micheli** from Italy, **Michal** and **Michalski** from Poland, and **Carmichael** from Scotland.

# 3. SPEAKING OF MICHAEL

When a name is as old and popular as Michael, it is only natural that things and places will be named after it. In fact, forms of the name have even become a part of our speech.

Michael is such a common name in Ireland that **Mike, Mick,** and **Mickey** have all been used as slang terms for an Irishman. Potatoes (Ireland's main food crop) were called **"mickies."** The **Mickey Finn** or **mickey**—a drink containing a drug that will knock its victim out—was named for a bartender who drugged his customers' drinks to help his thieving partners to rob them.

Some words are named after famous Michaels: the electrical unit called the **farad** after Michael Faraday, the **begonia** plant after Michel Begon, and the **Pippin apple** after Michael Henry Pippin. But some other common words that *seem* to be named after Michaels are just a coincidence—the use of **mike** as a short form for microphone, for example. **Mike and Ike** was a kind of rhyming nickname for salt and pepper shakers; today it is the brand name of a kind of candy.

Churches, mountains, and a popular street in Paris have been named after **St. Michael,** the archangel. His holiday, September 29, gave us the **Michaelmas daisy** and the **Michaelmas moon** (the harvest moon).

11

# 4. THE WORLD OF MICHAELS

He's an actor— an astronaut— a businessman— a doctor— a scientist— a singer— a sports star— a writer— Michaels have been leaders in many fields, and their varied lives are an inspiration to those who share their name.

## Once a King...

*Michael V of Romania (1921- )*
*- Romanian king, stockbroker -*

It's hard for an ex-king to find a job. **Michael V of Romania** knows that all too well—he has lost his crown twice. The first time he was declared King of Romania, he was just a child. When he was nine his father returned to power. But Michael regained the throne ten years later, only to lose his crown again when the communists took over after World War II. He went to Switzerland, married, and became a stockbroker. When Michael's father, Prince Carol, died, he left his son a huge fortune in a Swiss bank. But Prince Carol never gave Michael the code word he needs to get the money. A few times each year, Michael goes to the bank to try some new combinations. He also hopes that some-day he will be king of Romania again. "We live near the airport," he says, "just in case."

Michael Caine

*Michael Caine (1933- )*
- *British actor -*

Movie star **Michael Caine** literally fell into his acting career. While still in school, he was on his way to play basketball when he stopped for a peek at a girl named Amy in the drama class. He leaned too hard on the swing door and fell into the classroom. "Come on in," said the drama teacher. "We need some boys." "Nothing came of the thing with Amy," says Caine, "but I got hooked on acting." He studied acting for years while supporting himself with odd jobs, and landed many minor movie parts, before he proved himself with an Oscar nominated performance in the 1966 movie, *Alfie.* Michael Caine quickly went on to become a superstar, playing numerous roles, and received two more Oscar

nominations, and an Oscar for his performance in
*Hannah and Her Sisters* in 1985.

## Rising Star in Tennis

*Michael Chang (1972- )*
*- Chinese-American tennis player -*
There's a special excitement in the sports world when
a very young player becomes a star. Tennis fans discovered a new favorite in June 1989, when **Michael
Chang** entered the French Open. He had just turned pro
the year before, at the age of sixteen, and already he
was ranked No. 19 of all the tennis players in the
world. Michael was the youngest player ever to compete
in the French Open finals, and he won the tournament!
Michael's development has been guided by his father, a
research chemist who emigrated to the United States
from Taiwan. His dad still works closely with him,
helping to plan the strategies for his matches.

## Best-Selling Doctor

*Michael Crichton (1942- )*
*- American writer, director, physician -*
**Michael Crichton** graduated from Harvard Medical
School and did a year of medical research at the famous
Salk Institute, but then he decided not to practice med-
icine. Instead, he has used his medical knowledge to
write popular novels and movies, such as *The Andromeda
Strain, The Terminal Man,* and *Sphere.* The hit movies
he has directed include *Westworld* and *The Great Train
Robbery.* In addition to creating these fiction classics,

Michael Crichton

Michael Crichton has also written several nonfiction books and created a computer game called *Amazon.*

## A Man With a Heart

*Michael Ellis De Bakey (1908- )*
*- American cardiovascular surgeon -*

If our hearts stopped beating for more than a few minutes we would die. Yet surgeons can temporarily stop a damaged heart during an operation. Open-heart surgery would not be possible without the heart-lung machine, which takes over the work of sending blood through the body. Medical pioneer **Michael De Bakey** led the team that developed the pump for the heart-lung machine. He also started the use of Dacron tubes to replace damaged blood vessels and helped to prepare the way for the development of artificial hearts. Still active as a researcher in his eighties, Dr. De Bakey is known and respected all over the world.

# Talent Runs in the Family

*Michael Douglas (1944- )*
*- American actor, producer -*

It is hard to be the son of a famous father, especially when you are trying to make a career in the same field. People are always comparing: "Is he as good as his Dad?" **Michael Douglas** doesn't have to worry about that any more. His father, Kirk Douglas, was one of Hollywood's top stars for nearly forty years, but Michael has made a big name for himself. After starring in the popular TV series, *The Streets of San Francisco,* he tried producing a movie—and won an Oscar for *One Flew Over the Cuckoo's Nest* in 1976. He continued his acting, too: As the star of smash-hit films like *Romancing the Stone, Fatal Attraction,* and *Wall Street,* he soon became one of Hollywood's biggest box-office attractions. His performance in *Wall Street* won him the 1987 Academy Award as Best Actor.

# Greek-American Hero

*Michael Dukakis (1933- )*
*- American political leader -*

Massachusetts Governor **Michael Dukakis** was the Democratic Party's candidate for President of the United States in 1988. Many people were disappointed when he was defeated, but perhaps none more than the 650 people who live in the Greek village of Pelopi. Their main street is called Michael Dukakis Street, and the central square is M. Dukakis Square. To them this Greek

Michael Dukakis

immigrant's son is a hero who represents all the great possibilities of America. As governor of Massachusetts in the 1970s and 1980s, Michael Dukakis helped to turn the state's economy around, with record numbers of new jobs and record low unemployment levels.

## Mr. Electricity

*Michael Faraday (1791-1867)*
*- British physicist, chemist -*

**Michael Faraday** was one of the greatest scientists who ever lived, but he never had a formal education. His family was too poor to send him to school; instead, he was apprenticed to a bookbinder. Young Faraday read everything that came into the shop, and dreamed of becoming a scientist. After hearing a series of lectures by a famous scientist, Sir Humphrey Davy, Faraday sent a carefully prepared and bound set of lecture notes to Davy, along with a request for a job as a laboratory assistant. Sir Humphrey was impressed, and Faraday got the job. In the years that followed, Faraday made many important scientific discoveries. He is best known for his work in electricity and magnetism, which laid the groundwork for the development of electric motors, transformers, and ultimately our modern industrial world.

Michael J. Fox

## The Secret of His Success

*Michael J. Fox (1961- )*
*- Canadian actor -*

As a high school student, **Michael J. Fox** thought acting would be a good way to meet girls. Soon he discovered that he loved acting, and after some parts on

Canadian TV he moved to Los Angeles to pursue his career. It wasn't easy to break in. Small parts on TV series like *Trapper John* and *Lou Grant* didn't pay a steady income. The young actor lost twenty pounds living on macaroni and was selling off pieces of furniture to pay his debts when a big break finally came in 1982. He won a part in a new TV series, *Family Ties,* and helped to make it a hit. Then the lead in Steven Spielberg's movie, *Back to the Future,* made Fox one of Hollywood's hottest actors. His fans were thrilled in 1988 when he married his *Family Ties* sweetheart, Tracy Pollan.

## Friend of the Poor

*Michael Harrington (1928-1989)*
*- American college professor, activist -*

Homeless people have been in the news lately. With millions of Americans without homes, or just barely surviving, poverty is an important problem. It is not a new problem, though. Back in the 1960s, President John F. Kennedy became concerned about it when he read a book called *The Other America,* by **Michael Harrington**. Harrington first became aware of the "invisible land"—the poor people in America that most people never see or think about—when he was a social worker just out of college. "How long shall we look the other way while our fellow human beings suffer?" he asked in his book. In 1964, President Lyndon Johnson asked Michael Harrington to help set up a program called the War on Poverty. Till the end of his life, Harrington continued to fight for changes that could help wipe out poverty in America.

Michael Jackson

## Music's Thriller

***Michael Jackson** (1958- )*
*- American singer, songwriter, dancer, actor -*

Each day, **Michael Jackson**'s music album, *Thriller*, sets a new world record for the best-selling album ever. Since its release in 1982, *Thriller* has already sold more than 40 million copies! And that is just one highlight of an amazing career that started when Michael was only five years old. As the youngest member of the Jackson Five, he made music with his brothers that included seven platinum singles and three platinum albums. At thirteen, Michael made his first solo album, *Got to*

*Be There,* and it won him the title of male vocalist of the year. A later solo album, *Off the Wall,* sold more than 7 million copies and included four Top-Ten singles. That was a record for a solo album—until it was topped by Jackson's 1987 album, *Bad,* which had five number-one hits. This talented superstar does it all—he sings, dances, writes his own songs, and has even written a best-selling book about his life.

Michael Jordan

## Super Scorer

*Michael Jordan (1963- )*
*- American basketball player -*

Who is the best player in basketball today? Many sports fans say it is **Michael Jordan**. In fact, some sportswriters have called him the best basketball player ever. He has been a star since his first season as guard for the Chicago Bulls, in 1984-1985, when he out-scored everyone in the National Basketball League and was voted Rookie of the Year. Since then, this All-Star player has been the top scorer in the league nearly every season and has led the Bulls into the playoffs each year. In 1988 he was named the NBA's Most Valuable Player. Fans love to watch Michael Jordan's amazing moves and spectacular shots, and they fill the arenas wherever he plays.

## Behind Batman's Mask

*Michael Keaton (1951- )*
*- American actor -*

The big movie of 1989 was Batman. **Michael Keaton** was the dynamic star who played millionaire Bruce Wayne, otherwise known as Batman, Gotham City's most famous fighter of crime and injustice. Michael Keaton started out as a stand-up comic, and he used his comic talents in his first roles in TV series and movies like *Night Shift, Mr. Mom, Gung Ho,* and *Beetlejuice.* Comedians sometimes have a hard time convincing critics that they are good actors. In 1988 he proved he was a dramatic actor, too, with a highly praised performance as a drug addict in *Clean and Sober.* Then Batman came along, bringing him his biggest hit yet.

# 5. MICHAEL BY ANY OTHER NAME

Not all the notable Michaels of the world answer to "Michael." Some prefer a more informal Mickey or Mike. Some have variations like Mitchell, Mitch, Miles or Mick. Some, born in other lands, are named Michel, Michele, Miguel, Mikhail, or Misha.

Mike Schmidt

## Greatest Third Baseman

*Mike Schmidt (1949- )*
*- American baseball player -*
   Baseball fans elected **Mike Schmidt** to the National League All-Star Team in 1989—even though he had retired

in May of that year. To many baseball lovers, Mike is the best third baseman ever. His dozens of records include eight home run titles—tops for the National League. Schmidt hit a total of 548 home runs, seventh on the all-time list and the most for any third baseman in baseball history. Ten Gold Glove awards are proof of his outstanding defensive play. Voted the National League's Most Valuable Player three times, Schmidt played an amazing total of 2212 games—the most for any Major League third baseman.

## The Youngest Champ

*Mike Tyson (1966- )*
*- American heavyweight champion boxer -*

Mike Tyson grew up in a rough neighborhood in Brooklyn, New York, and he might have turned to drugs or crime. But a talented boxing teacher, Cus D'Amato, turned Mike's life around. He practically adopted Mike and taught him how to turn his raw force into boxing skill. All along, D'Amato had faith in Mike and predicted he would become the youngest heavyweight champ ever. Cus D'Amato died in 1985, but just one year later his dream came true when Mike Tyson, at the age of twenty, became the heavyweight champion of the world.

## Monkee-ing Around

*Mickey Dolenz (1945- )*
*- American singer, actor, TV director, producer -*

It seems like **Mickey Dolenz** was never just "monkee"-ing around. At the age of eleven, he was already an actor, starring in the TV series, *Circus Boy*. He continued his career with guest appearances on various television shows, but his real fame came in 1966, with a new rock group called The Monkees. The group started out as a TV show, patterned after a Beatles' film. For a few years The Monkees were very popular, but the group disbanded in the late 1960s, and Mickey Dolenz built up an independent career in acting, producing, and directing. Meanwhile, the old Monkees' songs were still being played and enjoyed by new generations of fans. In 1986 the group got together again for an anniversary tour, and their huge success proved that The Monkees were more than just a memory.

## The Commerce Comet

*Mickey Mantle (1931- )*
*- American baseball player -*

**Mickey Mantle**'s father was a real baseball fan. He named his son after Mickey Cochrane, a star catcher for the Detroit Tigers, and put a baseball in Mickey's crib. By the time the boy was two, he was out in the backyard with his father, learning to switch-hit. A football injury in high school almost ended Mickey's athletic career. He developed a serious bone infection and had to have five operations. The Yankees showed their faith in his recovery—and his talent—by signing him up straight out of high school. In 1951, the Yankee star Joe DiMaggio called Mickey "the greatest rookie I have ever seen." The kid from Commerce, Oklahoma, played for the Yankees for eighteen years and helped them win twelve pennants with his 536 career home runs. One of baseball's all-time greats, Mickey Mantle was elected to the Baseball Hall of Fame in 1971.

Mickey Rooney

## Still a Star

*Mickey Rooney (1920- )*
*- American actor -*

**Mickey Rooney** had his first role on the stage at the age of fifteen months, and he hasn't stopped acting since then. In the late 1930s he was the world's number one box office attraction. He played a typical teenager in the Andy Hardy series, and movie fans also loved his musicals with Judy Garland. When Mickey grew up, he played memorable roles in movies like *Breakfast at Tiffany's, The Black Stallion,* and *The Bridges of Toko-Ri.* In 1975 he said he was going to retire, but nobody believed him. Sure enough in 1979 he played the lead in a Broadway musical smash hit, *Sugar Babies.* The former child star is a senior citizen now, but he's still going strong in movies and on TV.

Miguel de Cervantes

## The Man of La Mancha

*Miguel de Cervantes Saavedra (1547-1616)*
*- Spanish writer -*

King Philip III of Spain once saw a man laughing hysterically at the book he was reading. "That man is either crazy," remarked the king, "or he is reading *Don Quixote.*" People have been laughing for nearly four centuries at the cockeyed adventures of the gallant knight who challenged windmills and imaginary evils. Don Quixote's creator, **Miguel de Cervantes**, lived a life that was just as varied and exciting. Cervantes fought bravely as a soldier, then was captured by pirates and sold as a slave. Safely home in Spain, he took a job as a tax collector but was soon thrown in jail because he couldn't keep his books balanced. In prison, Cervantes thought of the plot for *Don Quixote,*

27

the adventures of the "ingenious gentleman of La Mancha." He used his own experiences as the background for his comical story, and the novel was an instant success.

## Inventor of the Essay

*Michel Eyquem de Montaigne (1533-1592)*
*- French essayist, mayor -*

*Essay* means "an attempt" or "experiment," and that is what French writer **Michel de Montaigne** modestly called his writings. He set down his thoughts and views about life and questions that occurred to him while he was reading. At first he intended to write only for himself, but his essays—which eventually filled three thick volumes—were published and won many devoted readers. Montaigne's wit and ideas still seem fresh 400 years later, and writers of modern essays copy his personal approach and informal style.

## Did He Have ESP?

*Nostradamus (Michel de Notredame) (1503-1566)*
*- French astrologer, physician, clairvoyant -*

**Nostradamus** was trained as a doctor but soon found there was more money to be made in astrology. His book of predictions, *Centuries,* was published in 1555. Its words, written in verse, were so vague that people could read many different meanings into them. When King Henry II was killed suddenly in a tournament accident, a verse in *Centuries* seemed to predict the event, and Nostradamus became a celebrity. Today millions regard him as a prophet and search through his book for new insights. Some say he predicted the rise of Hitler and World War II; other verses seem to foretell another world war toward the end of this century.

Mikhail Baryshnikov

## Master of the Dance

*Mikhail Baryshnikov (1948- )*
*- Russian-American dancer, director, choreographer -*

Canadian ballet fans had an opportunity to watch a great Russian ballet company in 1974. But the Kirov ballet troupe's tour of Canada was an opportunity of another kind for star dancer **Mikhail Baryshnikov**. He defected from the Soviet Union, seeking a way to express his art more freely. Joining the American Ballet

Theater in New York, he thrilled audiences all over the world with his brilliant performances. In 1980 Mischa became the ABT's artistic director. Meanwhile, he has also starred in acting roles in movies, *The Turning Point* and *White Nights*. Still dancing, Mikhail Baryshnikov is helping to shape the careers of ballet stars of the future.

Mikhail Gorbachev

## "Man of the Decade"

*Mikhail Sergeyevich Gorbachev (1931- )*
*- Soviet political leader -*

One man can change the world. When **Mikhail Gorbachev** became the leader of the Soviet Union in 1985, his bold new ideas and policies surprised everyone. "It is like spring," said a Soviet writer, as Gorbachev built his programs of *glasnost* ("openness") and *perestroika* (a "rebuilding" and reform of the USSR economy). The Russian leader quickly became a worldwide hero, and his ideas spread through Europe. One after another, the

Communist countries of Europe began to form more democratic governments. Nations that had been enemies in the long Cold War now began to look for ways to work together peacefully. In 1989 *Time Magazine* named Mikhail Gorbachev "Man of the Decade"—the person who had the greatest impact on the world, not only for the 1980s but probably for many years to come.

Michelangelo

## Renaissance Man

*Michelangelo di Lodovici Buonarroti Simoni (1475-1564)*
*- Renaissance sculptor, painter, architect, poet -*

**Michelangelo**'s wealthy father didn't want his son to become an artist. But the boy was talented, and by the age of sixteen he was already working for Lorenzo the Magnificent, the ruler of Florence. During his long and productive life, Michelangelo became one of the leading figures in the Renaissance art world. He considered himself a sculptor, but he was also a successful architect, who worked for popes and princes and designed St. Peter's Cathedral in Rome. Michelangelo was a poet, too. But he is probably best remembered as a painter. Perhaps his greatest accomplishment is the huge panorama of Biblical scenes on the ceiling of the Sistine Chapel. This enormous work took four years to complete, lying on his back on scaffolds, just a few feet from the ceiling. Michelangelo never married. He said once that his art was his wife, and "my children shall be the works that I leave." They still live on.

## Rock'n'Roll Legend

*Mick Jagger (1944- )*
*- British singer -*

The Rolling Stones were a top British rock group in the 1960s, and after three decades they are still going strong. **Mick Jagger**, the group's lead singer, is one of the best known entertainers in the world. His career started with a chance meeting. He was on the way to class at the London School of Economics when he happened to meet an old friend from his neighborhood, Keith Richards. The two friends began talking about their love of American rock'n'roll and the blues, and soon they were thinking about starting their own band. With another guitar player, Brian Jones, they formed the Rolling Stones. Mick and Keith went on to write many classic hits together, including "Satisfaction," "Honky Tonk Women," and "Angie."

## A Musical Life

*Misha Dichter (1945- )*
*- American pianist -*

"I was lucky in not being a child prodigy," says pianist **Misha Dichter**. Although he had begun taking piano lessons at six, no one realized how talented he was until his mid-teens. So there was plenty of time during his growing-up years for hanging out with his surfer friends in Southern California. He made up for it later with long hours of practice, and in 1966 he launched his career by triumphing at the International Tchaikovsky Competition in Moscow. Even now, a musical superstar, Misha still practices 12 to 14 hours a day when he is learning a new piece, and averages over 100 performances a year. "I love it," he says, but he also finds time to play tennis, jog, and sketch.

## A Woman Named Michael

*Michael Learned (1939- )*
*- American actress -*

Popular actress **Michael Learned** isn't sure why her parents gave her a "boy's" name. "Maybe they thought it was a good joke," she once said. Her career certainly hasn't been a joke. She won three Emmy awards for Best Actress as Olivia Walton, the mother on the popular, long-running TV series, *The Waltons*, and then another Emmy for her leading role in the series, *Nurse*. Michael Learned returned to television in 1989 in another popular series, *Living Dolls*.

# 6. MICHAEL AS A LAST NAME

George Michael

## A Dream Come True

*George Michael (1963- )*
*- British singer, songwriter -*

When **George Michael** was seven years old, he knew he wanted to be a recording star. One of his earliest idols was Elton John; imagine the thrill Michael felt when Elton himself presented him with the Ivor Novello Award for best songwriter in Britain in 1985! Michael had started out with the group Wham!, formed with his childhood friend, Andrew Ridgeley. The group quickly rose to the top of the charts, and in 1985 Wham! was the first Western pop group ever to perform in China. George Michael left Wham! in 1986 for a solo career, and his 1987 hit album *Faith* had four number one songs. It even reached the top of *Billboard* magazine's black album chart—the first time ever for a white soloist.

## The Man Behind the Laughs

*Lorne Michaels (1944- )*
*- Canadian TV producer and writer -*

**Lorne Michaels** is the creator, producer, and writer of *Saturday Night Live*, one of the most popular comedy shows of the generation. He started out writing for *Rowan and Martin's Laugh-In* in the late 1960s. Since then he has written and produced specials for stars such as Lily Tomlin, Perry Como, Flip Wilson, the Beach Boys, Simon and Garfunkel, and Steve Martin—and picked up seven Emmy awards along the way! His occasional cameo appearances on *Saturday Night Live* are rare opportunities to see the man behind the laughs.

## Home Run Slugger

*Kevin Mitchell (1962- )*
*- American baseball player -*

Baseball star **Kevin Mitchell** grew up in a tough neighborhood in San Diego, where his brother was killed in a gang fight. Little League baseball kept Kevin off the streets and pointed the way to a better life. In the Big Leagues, he found a home with the Giants and began to show what he could really do. By the All-Star break in July of 1989, it looked like he had a chance to break Roger Maris' all-time home run record. He didn't, but he led the Majors that year with 47 home runs. "Without baseball," he said in an interview with *People Magazine*, "I'd probably be in jail or somewhere dead. ...But now kids can see me and say, 'There's something else we can do. Just look at Mitch.'"

# 7. MICHAEL FIRSTS

Archangel Michael

## The First Famous Michael

*Michael (Biblical times)*

Bible stories tell of several Michaels, but the most famous of all was an angel. **Michael** was God's special messenger. He brought the Ten Commandments to Moses and told the Virgin Mary about her coming death. Legends linked him to the beginning and the end of humanity's reign on earth. He gathered the dust from which Adam was created and will blow the horn to signal the Day of Judgment. Michael was a warrior, the general of God's armies. He constantly battled against his twin brother, Satan, the fallen angel who became the symbol of evil. For thousands of years, Michael has been revered by Jews, Christians, and Moslems as the greatest of all the angels.

# Watching Our Money

## Michael Hillegas (1729-1804)

How would you like to be in charge of all the money in the United States—and have your name on all the new bills printed, too? That's the job of the Treasurer of the United States. **Michael Hillegas,** a successful businessman, was appointed Treasurer of the United Colonies in 1775, a year before the Declaration of Independence was signed. During the Revolutionary War, he gave a large part of his wealth to support the fight for independence. In 1789, when the Treasury Department was formed, Hillegas became the nation's first Treasurer.

# Father of Russian Science

## Mikhail Vasil'evich Lomonosov (1711-1765)

**Mikhail Lomonosov** was a scientific genius whose theories in chemistry and physics were far ahead of his time. He was the first person ever to see the atmosphere of Venus, but no one outside of Russia knew about the discovery for 150 years. In fact, most of Lomonosov's discoveries remained unknown in the rest of the world, and other scientists got credit for them. Mikhail Lomonosov was a talented writer as well. He wrote the first history of Russia, and his works helped to shape the Russian language. He is still nearly unknown in the Western world, but in his homeland, Lomonosov is a famous scientific hero. The town where he was born, one of the greatest universities of the USSR, and even one of the craters on the moon now carry his name.

# 8. NICKNAMES

Michael Avallone

## The Fastest Typewriter in the East

*Michael Avallone (1924- )*

Many writers take months or even years to write a book—but not **Michael Avallone.** One year, he wrote 27 novels! All together, he has written more than 1000 published works, including 200 novels. Many writers write just one kind of book—but not Michael Avallone. "A professional writer should be able to write anything," he says, and he has written everything from detective stories to children's books, from movie reviews to poetry. Where does a writer get ideas for so many works? Avallone finds his in his diary, which he has been keeping since he was a teenager. He says that his most famous character, Detective Ed Noon, is the symbol of all the heroic things he dreamed of being when he was young.

# Air Jordan

*Michael Jordan (1963- )*

At six-foot-six, **Michael Jordan** is just a medium-sized basketball player. But he plays like a giant against the seven-footers in the National Basketball Association. He can score, set up plays, and leap into the air to snatch the ball away from his taller opponents. Admiring sportscasters call the Bulls' superstar **Air Jordan;** some of them call him **Superman in Shorts.**

# The Hero of New England

*Miles Standish (1584-1656)*

**Miles Standish** is probably the most famous jilted lover in history, thanks to Longfellow's famous poem, *The Courtship of Miles Standish.* Historians say there is no real evidence that Miles ever asked John Alden to propose to the lovely Priscilla for him. But there was nothing fictional about Standish's heroic service to the Pilgrim settlers of Plymouth colony. As their military leader, he saved them many times from attacks by unfriendly Indians. Short and stocky, Miles Standish was sometimes nicknamed the **Little Indian Fighter.** But the grateful settlers more often called him **The Hero of New England.** Today his statue stands in Duxbury, Massachusetts, overlooking Plymouth Bay where the *Mayflower* landed in 1620.

# 9. MEMORABLE MOMENTS

### A Bug's-Eye View

The great Russian-born dancer **Mikhail Baryshnikov** has danced and acted many roles, but probably the most unusual one was in a stage play in 1989. In the play, *Metamorphosis,* based on the novel by Franz Kafka, Baryshnikov starred as a man who wakes up one day to find he has turned into a cockroach!

### All Alone

Most people feel lonely sometimes, but they aren't really alone. With five billion people on earth, there is usually someone around to call if you need help. Imagine, though, what it must feel like to be *really* alone, 200,000 miles from home! That's how astronaut **Michael Collins** felt in 1969, while Neil Armstrong and Buzz Aldrin were making history by walking on the moon and he sat in his command module, circling above them. "I knew I was alone in a way that no earthling has ever been before."

### Grandparent's Day

Mother's Day and Father's Day are special holidays when children show their love and respect for their parents. But what about grandparents? Don't they deserve a special day of their own? That was the idea that came to **Michael Goldgar** when he was visiting an elderly aunt in a nursing home. A holiday just for grandparents would help to brighten their lives and bring back memories of a time when families were closer. Goldgar went to Washington and talked to people in Congress, asking them to declare a national Grandparent's Day. Over the next seven years, this determined grandfather spent eleven thousand dollars of his savings to make seventeen trips to Washington. Finally, in 1978, Congress passed a law establishing the Sunday after Labor Day as Grandparent's Day.

## Treasure Hunt

Many people dream about finding lost treasures of the past. That dream came true in 1985 for **Michael Hatcher.** He had been searching the ocean bottom for more than twenty years, bringing up cargoes from ships that sank during World War II. In the South China Sea he found the wreck of a far older ship—the Dutch *Geldermalsen,* which had sunk in 1752. Eighty of the 112 crew members went down with the ship. One of the survivors, boatswain Christoffer van Dijk, was accused of stealing the gold the ship carried and leaving the captain and crew to drown. The unlucky seaman was innocent, but no one believed him. More than two hundred years later, Michael Hatcher found the ship's cargo of gold, porcelain, and tea, and cleared the Dutchman's name. The treasure hunter gained a handsome reward when the gold and procelain sold at auction for twelve million dollars.

Michael Winner

## Sued by a Dog

In 1976, British director **Michael Winner** was best known as the director and producer of *Death Wish* and other Charles Bronson adventures, when he discovered he had another claim to fame. He was being sued by the estate of a dog! The suit claimed that his movie, *Won Ton Ton, the Dog That Saved Hollywood*, was really the life story of a famous Hollywood dog star, Rin Tin Tin, and Winner had made the film without getting permission from the dog's estate. Winner thought the situation was ridiculous. "It's absurd to be sued by a dog," he said, "especially by a dog who's been dead for the past twenty-five years."

# 10. MAKE-BELIEVE MICHAELS

Since Michael is such a popular name in the real world, it is not surprising that there are many Michaels in fiction as well—in stories, songs, books, plays, in the movies and on television.

## From Peter Pan to Doonesbury

It seems hard to believe that *Peter Pan* was first performed in 1904. This classic play has been a hit on the stage, in movies, and on TV. **Michael Darling** is one of the children that Peter Pan takes to Never Never Land. Some experts believe that the play's popularity sparked new interest in the name Michael, and also in Wendy, the name of Michael Darling's sister.

Another children's classic, *Mary Poppins*, tells about a magical housekeeper who comes to take care of **Michael Banks** and his sister in London. The book, by Pamela Travers, was made into an Oscar-winning movie.

For fifty years, young readers have been enjoying the story of **Mike Mulligan** *and His Steam Shovel.* Meanwhile, grownups have their own funny **Michael Doonesbury**, star of Gary Trudeau's popular comic strip. For forty years Mickey Spillane's hard-boiled private eye, **Mike Hammer**, has lived in best-selling novels, movies, and TV series.

Michaels have been featured in many popular TV series. **Mike Brady** was the idealized "TV dad" on *The Brady Bunch*, and the part of **Mike Seaver** in *Growing Pains* made Kirk Cameron a teen idol. In *Knight Rider,* **Michael Knight** crusaded against crime with a computerized talking Trans Am as his faithful sidekick. **Michael Steadman** helped keep things together on *Thirtysomething*, and **Mike Stratford** was the zany physician on *Doctor, Doctor.*

Musical Michaels range from the popular children's song, *Michael Finnigan,* who had "whiskers on his chin-i-gan," to the folksong **Michael** *Row the Boat Ashore,* and **Michael's** *Theme,* the theme song from *The Godfather.* The first movie theme song ever was **Mickey**, written for the 1918 silent film, *Mickey.*

## Fiction's Famous Mouse

Walt Disney's first cartoon "talkie" in 1928 featured **Mickey Mouse,** and he went on to star in over 100 films, which have been seen in nearly every country in the world. He has had his own comic strip, numerous Disney books, and his own TV show, *The Mickey Mouse Club.* He was featured as the Sorcerer's Apprentice in the movie, *Fantasia,* and even had his own day when Worcester, Massachusetts declared May 12 as "Mickey Mouse Day." His picture has appeared on millions of products, starting with Mickey Mouse watches. Mickey's popularity has helped to make the Disney empire a world leader.

# 11. MICHAEL SAYS:

"It's amazing how nice people are to you when they know you are going away." —**MICHAEL ARLEN**

"The essence of all art is to have pleasure in giving pleasure." —**MIKHAIL BARYSHNIKOV**

"A proverb is a short sentence based on a long experience." —**MIGUEL de CERVANTES**

"Here [in America] individuals of all nations are melted into a new race of men." —**MICHEL GUILLAUME JEAN de CREVECOUR**

"Love is the ultimate trip." —**MICKEY DOLENZ** *(in The Monkees)*

"The important thing is to know how to take all things quietly." —**MICHAEL FARADAY**

"If God had intended us to fly he would never have given us railways." —**MICHAEL FLANDERS**

"Concentrate on finding your goal, then concentrate on reaching it." —**COLONEL MICHAEL FRIEDSAM**

"Surely, God on high has not refused to give us enough wisdom to find ways to bring us an improvement...in relations between the two great nations on earth." —**MIKHAIL GORBACHEV**

"It's all right letting yourself go as long as you can let yourself back." —**MICK JAGGER**

"The game is my wife. It demands loyalty and responsibility, and it gives me back fulfillment and peace." —**MICHAEL JORDAN**

"Perched on the loftiest throne in the world, we are still sitting on our own behind."

"He who is not very strong in memory should not meddle with lying." —**MICHEL de MONTAIGNE**

"Behind every dark cloud, there's usually rain." —**MIKE NESMITH** (in *The Monkees*)

"The past is a foreign country. They do things differently there." —**MICHAEL REDGRAVE**

"It's unnatural for people to run around city streets unless they are thieves or victims. It makes people nervous to see someone running. I know that when I see someone running on my street, my instincts tell me to let the dog out after him." —**MIKE ROYKO**

"I've never been poor, but I've been broke. Being poor is a frame of mind. Being broke is only a temporary situation." —**MIKE TODD**

"If it weren't for the last minute, a lot of things wouldn't get done." —**MICHAEL S. TRAYLOR**

"A team effort is a lot of people doing what I say." —**MICHAEL WINNER**

# 12. NAME GAMES

## Who Said That?

Match these quotes to the Famous Michaels who said them:

1. "The essence of all art is to have pleasure in giving pleasure."

2. "Love is the ultimate trip."

3. "Behind every dark cloud, there's usually rain."

4. "The game is my wife."

5. "There are only two families in the world, the Haves and the Have-nots."

6. "It's all right letting yourself go as long as you can let yourself back."

A. Miguel de Cervantes

B. Mikhail Baryshnikov

C. Mick Jagger

D. Mickey Dolenz

E. Mike Nesmith

F. Michael Jordan

*Answers to Name Games on page 63.*

# Scrambled Michaels

These words and sentences are really people's names all jumbled up. Can you rearrange the letters to come up with a famous person named Michael? (Hint: Remove all punctuation.)

1. I'm a weak cell
2. As a duck like him
3. son-a-mustard
4. Handle no claim
5. Eek, moldy zinc!

6. Calm chain jokes
7. Yank melt mice
8. KID CHIMES™
9. Sink my toe
   My son tike
10. Chairman LegLeach

## CRYPTO-MICHAELS

These jumbled up letters really spell out a quote by a famous person named Michael. In each quote, every letter of the alphabet has been replaced by a different letter, and the substitution is consistent for the entire quote. If you dare, cover up the "Code" below, and try to "break it" yourself.

1. "LB ULY NQ GYS WBPX QSPYGO NG FBFYPX QLYIEC GYS FBCCEB UNSL EXNGO."
   —FNALHE CB FYGSKNOGB

2. "DSKDFKULPUF SK IRKNRKM WSHL MSPO, UGFK KSKDFKULPUF SK LFPDGRKM RU."
   —DSOSKFO CRDGPFO ILRFNEPC.

# Find That Michael

Can you find these ways of saying Michael in the puzzle below? (Hint: you can go up and down and diagonally.)

Micah, Michael, Michel, Michele, Mick, Mickey, Miguel Mikhail, Mihaly, Mika, Mike, Mikey, Miles, Milo, Mischa Misha, Mitchell:

|    | A | B | C | D | E | F | G | H | I | J |
|----|---|---|---|---|---|---|---|---|---|---|
| 1  | M | I | T | C | H | E | L | L | M | M |
| 2  | I | I | M | M | S | K | W | Z | I | I |
| 3  | X | L | K | I | T | I | X | M | S | K |
| 4  | H | E | N | H | U | M | Y | I | H | A |
| 5  | A | H | O | A | A | M | I | C | A | H |
| 6  | E | C | P | L | M | I | C | K | E | Y |
| 7  | L | I | Q | Y | V | L | L | A | E | C |
| 8  | J | M | I | C | H | E | L | E | B | Y |
| 9  | K | L | R | M | I | S | C | H | A | D |
| 10 | M | I | G | U | E | L | M | I | L | O |

# Michael Crossword Puzzle

## Across Clues

1. The Mickey Mouse ____.
3. Michael Jordan can really ____ with a basketball.
6. Michael Faraday helped pave the way for ____.
7. The Russian form of "Michael."
8. Michael Jackson's "Thriller" album was a real ____.
9. Jewel of the ____.
10. One of the first famous Michaels was an ____.
14. Michael V of Romania is an ____-King.
15. "Back ____ the Future."
16. Mike Schmidt hit a lot of these.
19. Michael Jackson, Michael Douglas, and Michael Caine are all ____.
21. Michael De Bakey is a doctor with a ____.

## Down Clues

2. One of Michael Keaton's best roles was as this superhero.
4. A first name that is also a last name.
5. You and ____.
7. This popular 60s music group had two Michaels in it.
11. One of Michael Jackson's trademarks is his white ____.
12. Mikhail Gorbachev is the leader of what country?
13. One of fiction's greatest animated heroes is a ____.
17. Mickey Mouse has big ____.
18. Michael Dukakis, Governor of ____.
20. Michael Landon can be seen in reruns on ____.

50

# JANUARY

| 1 | 2 | 3 | 4 | 5 | 6 | 7 |
|---|---|---|---|---|---|---|
| **Michael Owens,** 1859 (business) | **Sir Michael Tippett,** 1905 (composer) | **Michael Blumenthal,** 1926 (Gov. official) | | **Michael Macnamara,** 1925 (poet) | **Michael DiSalle,** 1908 (politician) | **Mike Liut,** 1956 (hockey) |
| 8 **Mike Reno,** 1955 (singer) | 9 | 10 **Michel Ney,** 1769 (military leader) | 11 **Mitchell Ryan,** 1928 (actor) | 12 **Michael Cook,** 1950 (poet) | 13 **Kevin Mitchell,** 1962 (baseball) | 14 **Michael Mandaziuk,** 1942 (artist) |
| 15 **Michel Debre,** 1912 (pol. leader) | 16 **Michael Simon White,** 1936 (producer) | 17 **Mick Taylor,** 1948 (musician) | 18 | 19 **Michael Crawford,** 1942 (actor) | 20 **Michel Bibaud,** 1782 (historian) | 21 **Mischa Elman,** 1891 (musician) |
| 22 **Mike Bossy,** 1957 (hockey) | 23 | 24 **Michael Ontkean,** 1946 (actor) | 25 **Michael Cotten,** 1950 (musician) | 26 | 27 **Mike Hill,** 1939 (golf) | 28 **Mikhail Baryshnikov,** 1948 (dancer) |
| 29 **Mike Foligno,** 1959 (hockey) | 30 **Mitch Leigh,** 1928 (composer) | 31 **Michel-Guillaume Jean Crèvecoeur,** 1735 (author) | | | | |

**Additional January Birthdays:**

15. **Mihail Eminescu,** 1850 "Romanian National Poet"
17. **Mack Sennett,** 1884 (director) "King of Comedy"

# FEBRUARY

| 1 | 2 | 3 | 4 | 5 | 6 | 7 |
|---|---|---|---|---|---|---|
| **Miguel Obando,** 1926 (rel leader) | | | **Michael Beck,** 1949 (actor) | **Mike Heath,** 1955 (baseball) | **Mike Farrell,** 1939 (actor) | |
| **8** **Michael Strong,** 1918 (actor) | **9** **Michael Kenn,** 1956 (football) | **10** | **11** | **12** **Mike Akiu,** 1962 (football) | **13** **Michel Bergerac,** 1932 (business) | **14** **Michael Cook,** 1933 (dramatist) |
| **15** **Michael Praetorius,** 1571 (composer) | **16** **Michael Harden,** 1959 (football) | **17** **Michael Jordan,** 1963 (basketball) | **18** **Michael Patrick Cleary,** 1939 (*Frank & Mike* radio show) | **19** **Mikolaj Kopernic (Copernicus),** 1473 (astronomer) | **20** **Mitch McConnell,** 1942 (politician) | **21** **Michael Field,** 1915 (musician) |
| **22** **Mike Oldfield,** 1953 (musician) | **23** **Mike Tresh,** 1914 (baseball) | **24** **Michael Harrington,** 1928 (activist) | **25** | **26** **Michael Bolton,** 1954 (singer) | **27** **Michael Calvello,** 1940 (poet) | **28** **Michel de Montaigne,** 1533 (writer) |

**February Michael Quote:**
"There are some defeats more triumphant than victories."
**Michel de Montaigne** (February 28)

# MARCH

| 1 | 2 | 3 | 4 | 5 | 6 | 7 |
|---|---|---|---|---|---|---|
| Michael Flanders, 1922 (actor) | Mikhail Gorbachev, 1931 (pol. leader) | | Mike Brown, 1959 (baseball) | Michael Warren, 1946 (actor) | Michelangelo, 1475 (artist) | Michael Eisner, 1942 (business) |
| **8** Mickey Dolenz, 1945 (actor, singer) | **9** Mickey Gilley, 1936 (musician) | **10** Michael Jacobs, 1880 (boxing promoter) | **11** | **12** | **13** | **14** Michael Caine, 1933 (actor) |
| **15** Mike Pagliarulo, 1960 (baseball) | **16** | **17** Michael O'Shea, 1906 (actor) | **18** Mike Webster, 1952 (football) | **19** | **20** Sir Michael Redgrave, 1908 (actor) | **21** |
| **22** Michael Hamburger, 1924 (poet) | **23** | **24** | **25** Michael Davitt, 1846 (revolutionary) | **26** Mike Loynd, 1964 (baseball) | **27** Michael York, 1942 (actor) | **28** Mike Fitzgerald, 1964 (baseball) |
| **29** Mike Kingery, 1961 (baseball) | **30** Mike Tilleman, 1944 (football) | **31** Mick Ralphs, 1948 (Musician) | | | | |

**Additional March Birthdays:**
9. Mickey Spillane, 1918 (writer)
14. Michael Gerald Ford, 1950 (son of Gerald Ford)
15. Mike Love, 1941 (singer-Beach Boys)
18. Michael Reagan, 1946 (son of Ronald Reagan)

# APRIL

| 1 | 2 | 3 | 4 | 5 | 6 | 7 |
|---|---|---|---|---|---|---|
| **Michael Johnson,** 1928 (poet) | | **Mischa Mischakoff,** 1895 (musician) | **Mike Haliwood,** 1940 (racer) | **Michael V Gazzo,** 1923 (actor) | **Mickey Cochrane,** 1903 (baseball) | **Mike Cofer,** 1960 (football) |
| **8** **Michael Bennett,** 1943 (choreographer) | **9** **Michael Learned,** 1939 (actress) | **10** **Mike Hawthorn,** 1929 (racer) | **11** **Michael "Sugar Ray" Richardson,** 1955 (basketball) | **12** **Michael Garrett,** 1944 (football/baseball) | **13** **Michael Brown,** 1941 (scientist) | **14** **Michael Parr,** 1927 (poet) |
| **15** **Michael Ansara,** 1922 (actor) | **16** | **17** **Michael Hendriks,** 1922 (poet) | **18** | **19** | **20** **Michel Leiris,** 1901 (writer) | **21** **Michel Goulet,** 1960 (hockey) |
| **22** | **23** | **24** **Mike Michalske,** 1903 (football) | **25** **Michael Stayt,** 1941 (poet) | **26** **Mike Scott,** 1955 (baseball) | **27** | **28** |
| **29** **Michael Ray Meadows,** 1961 (baseball) | **30** **Michael Smith,** 1945 (astronaut) | | | | | |

**Additional April Birthdays:**
6. **Michel Larocque,** 1952 (hockey)
26. **Michel Fokine,** 1880 (dancer)

# MAY

| 1 | 2 | 3 | 4 | 5 | 6 | 7 |
|---|---|---|---|---|---|---|
| | **Michael Rabin,** 1936 (musician) | | **Michael O. Myers,** 1943 (politician) | **Michael Palin,** 1943 (actor) | **Michel Stavaux,** 1948 (poet) | |
| **8** | **9** | **10** | **11** | **12** | **13** | **14** |
| **Mike Cueller,** 1937 (baseball) | **Mike Wallace,** 1918 (TV reporter) | **Mike Souchak,** 1927 (golf) | **Michael Heller,** 1937 (poet) | **Michael L Ainslie,** 1943 (business) | **Michael Welch,** 1940 (poet) | **Mike Quick,** 1959 (football) |
| **15** | **16** | **17** | **18** | **19** | **20** | **21** |
| **Michel Audiard,** 1920 (screenwriter) | **Michael Morris,** 1942 (artist) | | **(Michael) Shane Young,** 1962 (baseball) | **Michel Tsvett,** 1872 (scientist) | | **Michel Anatol Litvak,** 1902 (director) |
| **22** | **23** | **24** | **25** | **26** | **27** | **28** |
| **Michael Sarrazin,** 1940 (actor) | **Michel Deguy,** 1930 (poet) | **Mikhail Sholokhov,** 1905 (writer) | **Mischa Levitzki,** 1898 (musician) | **Michael Benedikt,** 1937 (writer) | **Mike "Pinky" Higgins,** 1908 (baseball) | **Michael Brown,** 1940 (poet) |
| **29** | **30** | **31** | | | | |
| | **Mikhail Bakunin,** 1814 (anarchist) | | | | | |

**May Michael Quote:**
"Liberty is indivisible." **Mikhail Bakunin** (May 30)

| J U N E | 1 | 2 | 3 | 4 | 5 | 6 | 7 |
|---|---|---|---|---|---|---|---|
| | **1**<br>Mikhail Glinka, 1804 (composer) | **2** | **3** | **4**<br>Mike Weaver, 1952 (boxer) | **5**<br>Mike Wise, 1964 (football) | **6** | **7** |
| | **8**<br>Michael Codron, 1930 (producer) | **9**<br>Michael J. Fox, 1961 (actor) | **10**<br>Mike Kreevich, 1908 (baseball) | **11**<br>Michael Cacoyannis, 1922 (director) | **12** | **13**<br>Michael Wright, 1938 (businessman) | **14**<br>Michael Andrews, 1939 (writer) |
| | **15**<br>Michel Lotito, 1950 (entertainer) | **16** | **17**<br>Mickey Brantley, 1961 (baseball) | **18** | **19**<br>Mishel Piastro, 1891 (musician) | **20**<br>Michael Anthony, 1955 (musician) | **21**<br>Michael Gross, 1947 (actor) |
| | **22**<br>Mike Todd, 1907 (producer) | **23**<br>Michael Shaara, Jr., 1929 (author) | **24** | **25**<br>George Michael, 1963 (singer) | **26**<br>Mike Griffin, 1957 (baseball) | **27** | **28** |
| | **29**<br>Micky Arison, 1949 (business) | **30**<br>Michael Whalen, 1902 (actor) | | **Michael Trivia**<br>What two June Michaels were both on a popular TV series together? | | | |

Michael J. Fox, Michael Gross in *Family Ties.*

# JULY

| 1 | 2 | 3 | 4 | 5 | 6 | 7 |
|---|---|---|---|---|---|---|
| Mike Tyson, 1966 (boxer) | | Mike Corby, 1955 (singer) | Mitch Miller, 1911 (musician) | Michael Gismondi, 1955 (musician) | Michael Novak, 1935 (poet) | |
| 8 Mike Ramsey, 1960 (baseball) | 9 Michael Graves, 1934 (architect) | 10 Mike Connolly, 1915 (journalist) | 11 | 12 Michael Kampen, 1939 (artist) | 13 Mickey Walker, 1901 (boxer/artist) | 14 Mike Lewis, 1949 (football) |
| 15 Mike Shannon, 1939 (baseball) | 16 | 17 Mitchell Wilson, 1913 (author) | 18 Mike Roy, 1912 (chef) | 19 | 20 Mike Witt, 1960 (baseball) | 21 Mike Hegan, 1942 (baseball) |
| 22 Michael Romanov, 1596 (Czar) | 23 Michael Foot, 1913 (politician) | 24 | 25 | 26 Mick Jagger, 1944 (singer) | 27 Michael Longley, 1939 (poet) | 28 Mike Bloomfield, 1944 (musician) |
| 29 Michael Spinks, 1956 (boxer) | 30 Michael Morris, Lord Killanin, 1914 (Olym. official) | 31 Mike Bielecki, 1959 (baseball) | | | | |

**Additional July Birthdays:**
4. Mickey Welch, 1859 (baseball -invented screwball)
20. Mike Ilitch, 1929 (owns Little Caesar's Pizza, Detroit Red Wings hockey team)

57

# AUGUST

| 1 | 2 | 3 | 4 | 5 | 6 | 7 |
|---|---|---|---|---|---|---|
| Michael Stewart, 1929 (playwright) | Michael Dailey, 1938 (artist) | Mackey Sasser, 1962 (baseball) | | | Michael Anderson, Jr., 1943 (actor) | Michael Smurfit, 1936 (business) |
| **8** Michael Collie, 1929 (poet) | **9** Michael Halberstam, 1932 (author) | **10** Michael Dokes, 1958 (boxer) | **11** Mike Douglas, 1925 (TV host) | **12** Michael Kidd, 1919 (dancer) | **13** | **14** Michael Abercrombie, 1912 (scientist) |
| **15** Mike Connors, 1925 (actor) | **16** | **17** Mikhail Botvinnik, 1911 (chess) | **18** Mike Lavalliere, 1960 (baseball) | **19** (Michael) Anthony Muoz, 1958 (football) | **20** | **21** Mickey Shuler, 1956 (football) |
| **22** | **23** Mike Boddicker, 1957 (baseball) | **24** Mike Black, 1964 (football) | **25** Michael Brownstein, 1943 (poet) | **26** Mike Farmer, 1936 (basketball) | **27** Mike Maddux, 1961 (baseball) | **28** Michael Chekhov, 1891 (director) |
| **29** Michael Jackson, 1958 (singer) | **30** Mike J. Bell, 1957 (football) | **31** Michel Chevreul, 1786 (scientist) | | | | |

**MICHAEL Trivia**

Mike Douglas (Aug 11) won the first Emmy ever given to a talk show host.

Choreographer Michael Kidd (Aug 12) won 5 Tony Awards including one for the classic "Hello Dolly."

# SEPTEMBER

| | | | | | | |
|---|---|---|---|---|---|---|
| **1**<br>Michael Smith, 1942 (poet) | **2** | **3** | **4** | **5**<br>Mikhail Kutuzov, 1745 (field marshal) | **6**<br>Mike McCoy, 1948 (football) | **7**<br>Dr. Michael De Bakey, 1908 (physician) |
| **8**<br>Michael J. Quill, 1905 (labor leader) | **9**<br>Michael Keaton, 1951 (actor) | **10**<br>Mike O'Callaghan, 1929 (politician) | **11**<br>Michel Jobert, 1921 (diplomat) | **12**<br>Mickey Lolich, 1940 (baseball) | **13**<br>Mike Fischlin, 1955 (baseball) | **14**<br>Michel Butor, 1926 (writer) |
| **15** | **16**<br>Mike Tettleton, 1960 (baseball) | **17**<br>Mike Current, 1945 (football) | **18**<br>Michael Hartnett, 1941 (poet) | **19**<br>Mike Royko, 1932 (journalist) | **20** | **21**<br>(Michael) Troy Afenir, 1963 (baseball) |
| **22**<br>Michael Faraday, 1791 (scientist) | **23**<br>Mickey Rooney, 1920 (actor) | **24**<br>Mike Gonzalez, 1890 (baseball) | **25**<br>Michael Douglas, 1944 (actor) | **26**<br>Mike Bragg, 1946 (football) | **27**<br>Mike Schmidt, 1949 (baseball) | **28**<br>Michelangelo da Caravaggio, 1573 (artist) |
| **29**<br>Miguel de Cervantes, 1547 (writer) | **30**<br>Michael Powell, 1905 (director) | | **Additional September Birthdays:**<br>19. Mika Waltari, 1908 (writer)<br>27. Misha Dichter, 1945 (musician)<br>29. Archangel Michael, (feast day) | | | |

# OCTOBER

| 1 | 2 | 3 | 4 | 5 | 6 | 7 |
|---|---|---|---|---|---|---|
| Michael Haider, 1904 (business) | Michael Rutherford, 1950 (musician) | Michael Hordern, 1911 (actor) | Michael Pupin, 1858 (scientist) | | Mike Haight, 1962 (football) | |
| 8 | 9 | 10 | 11 | 12 | 13 | 14 |
| Michael Korda, 1933 (editor) | Mike Singletary, 1958 (football) | | Mike Guerra, 1912 (baseball) | Miles Batt, 1933 (artist) | Mike Capel, 1961 (baseball) | Michael Sloan, 1946 (writer) |
| 15 | 16 | 17 | 18 | 19 | 20 | 21 |
| Mikhail Lermontov, 1814 (writer) | Michael Conrad, 1927 (actor) | Michael McKean, 1947 (actor) | Michael Wigglesworth, 1631 (poet) | Miguel Asturias, 1899 (writer) | Mickey Mantle, 1931 (baseball) | |
| 22 | 23 | 24 | 25 | 26 | 27 | 28 |
| | Michael Crichton, 1942 (writer) | | Michael V, 1921 (King) | | Michael Avallone, 1924 (writer) | |
| 29 | 30 | 31 | | | | |
| Michael Jayston, 1936 (actor) | Michael Winner, 1935 (director) | Michael Collins, 1930 (astronaut) | | | | |

**Additional October Birthdays:**
20. Michael McClure, 1932 (poet)
31. Michael Landon, 1936 (actor)

# NOVEMBER

| 1 | 2 | 3 | 4 | 5 | 6 | 7 |
|---|---|---|---|---|---|---|
| Mike Jensen, 1934 (news correspondent) | Mike Hamby, 1962 (football) | Michael Dukakis, 1933 (politician) | | | Mike Nichols, 1931 (director) | Mike Clark, 1940 (football) |
| **8** Mikhail Lomonosov, 1711 (scientist) (old calendar) | **9** Mikhail Ippolitov-Ivanov, 1859 (composer) | **10** | **11** Michael Metrinko, 1946 (Iran hostage) | **12** Sunset Carson (Michael Harrison), 1922 (actor) | **13** | **14** Mike Livingston, 1945 (football) |
| **15** Michel Chasles, 1793 (mathematician) | **16** Michael Arlen, 1895 (writer) | **17** Lorne Michaels, 1944 (producer) | **18** Mike Felder, 1962 (baseball) | **19** Mikhail Lomonosov, 1711 (scientist) | **20** Mikhail Kalinin, 1875 (politician) | **21** Mikhail Suslov, 1902 (politician) |
| **22** Michael Callan, 1935 (actor) | **23** | **24** | **25** | **26** Michael Butler, 1926 (business) | **27** Mike Scioscia, 1958 (baseball) | **28** |
| **29** Michael Kermoyan, 1925 (actor) | **30** Michael Walter, 1960 (football) | | | | | |

**November Michael Quote:**
''Nerves provide me with energy. They work for me. It's when I don't have them, when I feel at ease, that I get worried.'' **Mike Nichols** (November 6)

61

| | 1 | 2 | 3 | 4 | 5 | 6 | 7 |
|---|---|---|---|---|---|---|---|
| **D** | Michael Sovern, 1931 (educator) | | Mike Ramsey, 1960 (hockey) | | | Mike Baab, 1959 (football) | Michael Cudahy, 1841 (merchant) |
| **E C** | Michael Mott, 1930 (poet) — 8 | Michael Quinlan, 1944 (business) — 9 | Michael Manley, 1923 (pol leader) — 10 | Mike Heneman, 1961 (baseball) — 11 | Miguel de la Madrid, 1934 (pol leader) — 12 | Mike Mosley, 1944 (racing) — 13 | Michel de Notredame (Nostradamus), 1503 (astrologer) — 14 |
| **E M** | 15 | Mike Flanagan, 1951 (baseball) — 16 | Michel Velmans, 1926 (poet) — 17 | Michael Park, 1941 (poet) — 18 | Miguel Pinero, 1946 (dramatist) — 19 | Michael Hefferna, 1942 (poet) — 20 | Michael Thomas, 1944 (conductor) — 21 |
| **B E** | Michael Rutherford, 1946 (poet) — 22 | Mikhail Kalatozov, 1903 (director) — 23 | Mike Curb, 1944 (politician) — 24 | Mike Mazurki, 1909 (actor) — 25 | 26 | Mickey Redmond, 1947 (hockey) — 27 | 28 |
| **R** | Mike Lucci, 1940 (football) — 29 | Mike Nesmith, 1942 (musician) — 30 | Miguel de Unamuno, 1864 (philosopher) — 31 | | | | |

**December Michael Quote:**
"The greatest height of heroism to which an individual, like a people can attain is to know how to face ridicule." **Miguel de Unamuno** (Dec. 31)

*Trivia Answers*

## Who Said That? (p. 47) 1) B 2) D 3) E 4) F 5) A 6) C

## Scrambled Michaels (p. 48)

1. Mike Wallace    2. Mike Dukakis    3. Nostradamus
4. Michael Landon    5. Mickey Dolenz    6. Michael Jackson
7. Mickey Mantle    8. Mike Schmidt    9. Mike Tyson
10. Archangel Michael

## Crypto-Michaels (p. 48)

1. "He who is not very strong in memory should not meddle with lying." —Michel de Montaigne
2. "Concentrate on finding your goal, then concentrate on reaching it." —Colonel Michael Friedsam.

## Find That Michael (p. 49)

MICAH 5F,5G,5H,5I,5J

MICHEL 8B,7B,6B,5B,4B,3B

MICK 3H,4H,5H,6H

MIGUEL 10A,10B,10C,10D,10E,10F

MIKA 1J,2J,3J,4J

MIKEY 4F,5G,6H,7I,8J

MILES 5F,6F,7F,8F,9F

MISCHA 9D,9E,9F,9G,9H,9I

MITCHELL 1A,1B,1C,1D,1E,1F,1G,1H

MICHAEL 1A,2A,3A,4A,5A,6A,7A

MICHELE 8B,8C,8D,8E,8F,8G,8H

MICKEY 6E,6F,6G,6H,6I,6J

MIHALY 2D,3D,4D,5D,6D,7D

MIKE 4F,3F,2F,1F

MIKHAIL 1A,2B,3C,4D,5E,6F,7G

MILO 10G,10H,10I,10J

MISHA 1I,2I,3I,4I,5I

## Crossword Puzzle (p. 50)

# AN INDEX OF MICHAELS

# MICHAEL Honor Roll

Michael Dudley Alger 12/26/69
Michael Fitzgerald Akins 3/9/77
Michael John Atkinson 3/14/88
Michael Eric Beautz 6/25/72
Michael Vandyke Behling 12/9/87
Michael Craig Bolt 7/10/85
Michael David Booth 2/23/76
Michael Shane Bowles 10/10/75
Michael Philip Brien 10/19/55
Michael (Stanley) Thomas Bruning 8/5/70
Michael David Burch 9/24/81
Michael Anthony Cairone 2/3/83
Michael William Carlin 10/15/86
Michael John Carney 12/5/81
Michael Casey 6/4/53
Michael C. Casini 6/29/81
Michael Barry Cassell 12/27/83
Michael Anthony Cisero 2/25/78
Michael Joy Cohen 5/7/70
Michael Robert Conklin 2/11/88
Michael V. Campbell III 3/3/86
Michael Dean Chancellor 3/6/85
Michael Allen Cioffi 4/26/67
Michael J. Cook III 1/14/55
Michael J. Cook Jr. 4/17/08
Michael Christopher McCray Cromartie 7/13/87
Michael Thomas Daniels 2/8/87
Michael Keith Davis 2/6/78
Michael Demri 6/10/84
Michael Charles De Zaruba 9/23/86
Michael Donald Dopslaff 11/6/82
Michael Jay Douglass 7/6/80
Michael Joseph Drier 12/19/81
Michael Drosdowich 10/5/60
Michael Jay Embree 7/25/76
Michael Joseph Figura 10/3/81
Michael John Finnerty 8/8/78
Michael Anthony Fonner 10/29/86
Michael Richard Frank 4/27/82
Michael Shawn Garmon 4/17/77
Michael Drake Gauntlett 2/20/80
Michael Lee Geer 2/13/82
Michael R. Gibson 9/1/72
Michael Devin Gooch 7/11/50
Michael Scott Greenwald 1/13/75
Michael Grenier 11/21/87
Michael William Hart 1/3/73
Michael Scott Helms 6/5/85
Michael James Hesemann 3/30/88
Michael Anthony Hobocan 6/6/81
Michael Benjamin Ingram 9/1/84
Michael Anthony Jarrell 3/2/82
John Michael Johnson 8/4/65
Michael Gordon Kraft 3/14/81
Michael John Kryvanis 9/1/80
Michael Sean Laisney 1/30/74
Michael Leon Laskaris
Michael David Leach 6/18/77
Michael Paul Lindermuth 3/28/90
Michael Aaron Lipson 7/26/86
Michael David Logue 3/15/86

Michael Robert Lowden 10/14/86
Michael Anthony Macia 8/30/86
Michael Mangarella 7/23/88
Michael David Marshall 10/19/81
Michael Angelo McCray 2/2/60
Michael Fitzpatrick McGinn 6/5/82
Michael Francis McGrath 5/15/49
Michael Aidan McLeod 10/29/88
Michael Lee Miller 10/8/66
Michael Max Minick 3/5/73
Michael Andrew Moeller 4/18/90
Michael John Molleur 11/15/66
Michael Joseph Monahan 11/2/81
Michael John Morris 9/17/87
Michael David Mulford 7/10/78
Michael David Nelson 9/16/70
Michael Nicholas Nibler 8/31/84
Michael Scott Phillips 7/23/73
Michael Eugene Pittman 7/25/57
Michael Allen Poole 11/7/79
Michael Brendan Provencher 6/9/79
Michael Stephen Ray 12/26/69
Michael Mercedes Rice 5/6/84
Michael Joseph Rizzo 6/7/78
Michael John Ross
Michael Seeley Russell 3/23/88
Michael Louis Saltzman 3/31/68
Michael Joseph Savard 5/5/82
Michael Ben Shader 6/22/59
Michael Gary Shea 5/23/83
Michael Marie Sickmann 11/8/89
Michael Tyler Silberstein 4/25/80
Michael William Simpson 7/7/79
Michael Christopher Smith 1/2/87
Michael Joseph Smith Jr. 4/8/76
Michael Allen Springham 11/1/88
Michael Gary Stake 5/18/75
Michael Christopher Stone 6/28/79
Mikael Lee Sundin
Mikael Arthur Sundin
Michael Tetrick 12/15/69
Michael Wayne Thrailkill 12/28/68
Michael James Turri 10/9/76
Michael Anthony Tvardzik 10/21/89
Michael John Ulatoski Jr. 12/17/89
Michael Stephen Vashlishan 9/29/89
Michael Gerard Verian 10/5/64
Michael Joseph Visconti
Michael Dean Waas 12/31/76
Michael Clifford Wakelee, Jr. 12/17/89
Michael John Walsh 11/11/87
Michael Kilby Felton Weber 3/28/79
Michael George White 10/27/77
Michael James White 10/12/87
Michael John Williams 12/10/82
Michael Paul Williamson 9/13/84
Michael Brown Wisniewski 1/15/89
Michael Alfred Woods 5/20/83
Michael Joseph Yanovitch 8/10/89
Michael Clayton Yuen 7/26/88

## CALLING ALL MICHAELS

If you—or a Michael you know—would like to be included in the MICHAEL Honor Roll in future editions of the book, just send your name and address, together with the *full name and birthdate* of the Michael to appear in the Honor Roll to:

Honor Roll
AVSTAR Publishing Corp.
P.O. Box 537
Lebanon, NJ 08833

We're calling all JOHNS, MARYS, ROBERTS, ELIZABETHS, WILLIAMS, and KATHYS (or CATHYS), too, for the Honor Rolls in forthcoming books dedicated to those names.

Look for these AVSTAR books by the Silversteins:

*JOHN, Your Name Is Famous* (230 pg hardcover) .. $14.95
*JOHN* (63 pg quality paperback) ............... $ 4.95
*Lyme Disease, The Great Imitator*
   (126 pg hardcover) ......................... $12.95
   (126 pg quality paperback) .................. $ 5.95
*MICHAEL*
   (64 pg hardcover) .......................... $11.95
   (64 pg quality paperback) ................... $ 4.95

Available November 1990
*MARY* (63 pg quality paperback) ............... $ 4.95
*ROBERT* (63 pg quality paperback) ............. $ 4.95
*ELIZABETH* (63 pg quality paperback) .......... $ 4.95

Check your local bookstore for these fine publications, or order direct from the publisher:

AVSTAR Publishing Corp.
Box 537
Lebanon, NJ 08833
Tel.: (908) 236-6210

Please print your name and shipping address clearly and enclose a check, money order, or charge card information. (No CODs, please.)

On charge orders, please include the complete VISA or MasterCard number and expiration date.

Please add $2.00 for shipping and handling per order. (Order 1, 2, or 100 books and pay only $2 shipping!)